Breastfeeding 101

Breastfeeding 101

A Step-by-Step Guide to Successfully Nursing Your Baby

Expanded and revised second edition

Sue Tiller, R.N.
International Board Certified Lactation Consultant

Illustrations by Mary Ellen Didion-Carsley

TLC Publishing

Manufactured in the United States of America
Library of Congress Control Number: 2004098630
ISBN: 0-9721517-1-0
Book design and production by Tabby House
Cover design: Incite, graphic designs
Second edition

Disclaimer

This publication contains the opinions and ideas of the author and is designed to
inform and educate. It is not meant to be the sole source of breastfeeding information for the reader. This publication is not intended to diagnose or treat any
conditions in the mother or baby requiring medical intervention. Statements made
by the author do not constitute an endorsement of any product, service or organization by the author or publisher. Neither the author nor publisher shall have any
liability or responsibility to any person or entity with respect to any loss or damage caused or alleged to be caused, directly or indirectly, by the information
contained in this book.

TLC Publishing
5221 Rushbrook Drive
Centreville, VA 20120
www.breastfeeding101.com

Dedication

To my three wonderful daughters, for whom I wish I had the breastfeeding knowledge I now possess. The information I share with you would have made my personal breastfeeding experiences a little less bumpy and a little more lengthy.

Contents

Foreword

Pediatricians and obstetricians need a book on breastfeeding to recommend to their prenatal patients. *Breastfeeding 101* by Sue Tiller is that book. It is a focused, accurate, no-nonsense easy-to-read breastfeeding primer. Mothers are often intimidated by the need to succeed at breastfeeding. The mysteries of latch-on, cluster feeding and frequency of feeding are explained. Obstacles to nursing such as: breast engorgement, breast infections, sore nipples and thrush are addressed, as well as when it is time to ask for help from the physician and lactation consultant.

A clear and concise section on when to introduce the bottle, the art of pumping and the storage of breast milk allay the natural anxiety and stress of returning to work.

Breastfeeding 101 is a must for expectant mothers, nursing mothers, lactation consultants, La Leche Leaders, medical students and residents, nursing students, nurses, pediatricians, family practitioners, obstetricians and midwives.

Thomas J. Sullivan, M.D.
President, Virginia Chapter
American Academy of Pediatrics

Introduction

Congratulations on the birth of your baby. Breastfeeding is one of the most important things you can do for your baby. The nutrients and anti-infective properties in breastmilk are unmatched in formula and contribute greatly to promoting and maintaining your baby's health. In addition, there are benefits to you, the nursing mother, which include reduction in the rates of certain types of breast, uterine and ovarian cancers as well as a reduction in the risk of osteoporosis and a more rapid return to pre-pregnancy weight.

Throughout my twenty-five-plus years of assisting new moms with breastfeeding I've found the same comments and concerns arising again and again:

"Each time someone came to help me in the hospital I was told something different."

"Breastfeeding books are too long and filled with conflicting or confusing information."

"None of this makes any sense."

"Why does it seem to be so difficult for me?"

"I thought this would be so natural."

"I called my baby's pediatrician and they told me not to worry, the baby would catch on."

"Mom said, 'I didn't breastfeed you and you're just fine, what's all the hoopla about breastfeeding anyway? It just adds to your stress and confusion.' "

Many parents feel unprepared for the demands of a new baby. Difficulties with breastfeeding can feel magnified during this time of sleep deprivation as you navigate your role as a new parent. Since your newborn will need to eat often, difficulties with breastfeeding cannot be ignored.

Help is available. This book is designed as a quick reference for assistance with the initial hurdles in breastfeeding. It is not meant to take the place of a lactation consultation or a visit with or phone call to your baby's pediatrician.

This book provides short and concise steps on initiating breastfeeding in an easy-to-remember format. There is no one right way to breastfeed. Moms and babies are all different. So the method that works for you may not be good for your friend or even your next baby. But the guidelines and suggestions in this book can help you get off to a good start. I cannot emphasize this enough: *If difficulty persists, call for help.* Breastfeeding experts are out there! Use them, but don't forget to keep your pediatrician informed about what's going on.

Again, congratulations on your new baby. By obtaining good information you are starting off on the right track. Every day you breastfeed your baby, the benefits for both of you will last a lifetime.

1

Benefits of Breastfeeding

Breastmilk is the perfect food for your baby. Below is a list of some of the benefits you and your baby will enjoy when you choose to breastfeed.

- Your milk is the perfect nutrition for your baby. It changes in nutrients as your baby grows.[1]

- Breastmilk transfers antibodies from you to your baby to reduce illness and helps develop your baby's immune system.[2]

- Breastfeeding decreases the chances of ear infections by 3 to 4 times that of a formula-fed baby.[3]

- Breastfeeding decreases the risk of Sudden Infant Death Syndrome (SIDS).[4]

- Breastfed babies suffer less reflux (spit-up) than formula-fed babies.[5]

- Breastmilk decreases the chance of your baby developing asthma when she is older.[6]

- You will lose pregnancy weight more quickly. Making breastmilk uses 940 calories per liter.[7]

- Your uterus will return to its pre-pregnancy position more quickly. The hormone oxytocin is released as your baby suckles. This hormone releases the milk your breasts have produced. It also contracts your uterus to return it to its pre-pregnancy state.[8]

- Breastfeeding reduces the risk of certain types of breast, uterine and ovarian cancers. The longer you breastfeed, the more the risk is reduced.[9]

- Breastfeeding decreases the risk of developing osteoporosis for you and your baby.[10]

- Breastfeeding is more convenient than formula feeding. There is no need to prepare, heat, or clean bottles. It is always available at the right temperature.

- Breastfeeding is free.

2

Getting Started: Latch-on

This section provides an easy-to-remember way to start successful breastfeeding, using step-by-step instruction and illustrations that cover the basic latch-on process.

Latch-on comes easily for many babies, but some need a little more help. There are four basic positions: cross-cradle, football, cradle, and lying down. For most moms, cross-cradle and football are the easiest to learn when breastfeeding is just getting started. Once you and your baby have learned how to breastfeed the cradle and lying down positions will come more easily. *Breastfeeding 101* will teach the cross-cradle and football positions.

1. Sit in a chair because nursing in bed is harder in the beginning for most moms. The chair should have good support with a firm back and seat, armrests low enough to allow your elbows to rest comfortably and wide enough to tuck a pillow on your side for a football hold. You may want your feet on a small stool to ease strain on your back and to position baby closer to you.

2. Skin-to-skin contact between mother and baby can be very helpful for cueing baby's feeding instincts. Undress baby except for a diaper and open or remove your shirt as well. Some women prefer to keep their nursing bra on if the support it provides feels more comfortable. Avoid pulling your shirt up and holding it under your chin or pushing it out of the way.

3. Position your baby so her mouth is at your nipple level; use pillows to help support baby in this position. A firm, crescent-shape nursing pillow can be very helpful.

Cross-Cradle Position

Turn your baby on her side with her bottom arm around you, then bring her close to you so you are tummy to tummy.

For nursing the right breast, hold the base of her head firmly with your left hand. Your fingers should be around the sides of her head just behind her ears.

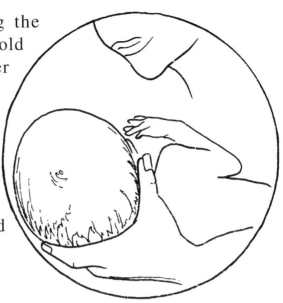

areola

Hold your right breast with your right hand, making a "**U**" shape about **2 inches** behind the nipple. This may or may not be on the edge of your areola (the darker area around the nipple), since areola come in many sizes. Your baby needs to grasp your nipple and about **1 inch** of areola to be fully latched-on.

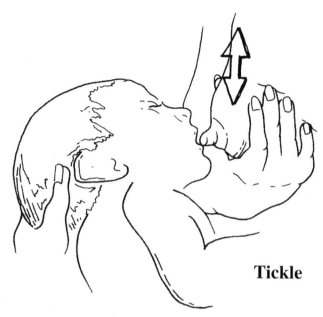

Tickle

Stroke your baby's lips from top to bottom with your nipple.

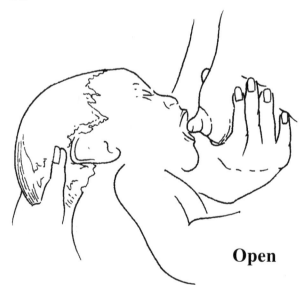

Open

When she responds with a *wide*-**open mouth**, use your hand behind her head to bring her *quickly* onto the breast.

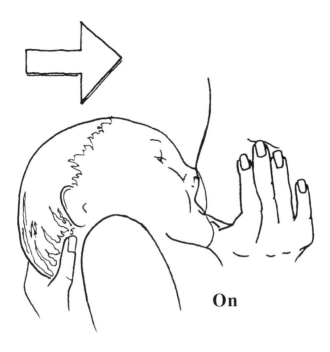

On

    An easy way to remember these three steps is "Tickle-Open-On." For nursing the left breast, use your right hand on your baby's head and your left hand on your left breast.

Tickle-Open-On
Since your baby's mouth will close quickly once something touches his lips, a quick motion is needed to be sure the nipple *and* areola are *both* latched. A slower motion usually results in the baby closing on just the nipple. (Ouch!)

Once your baby is properly latched, slowly release your right hand from your breast and cradle this arm around your baby. This arm position should be comfortable for you and provide support for your baby's head. Use your opposite hand to support your breast if needed.

Adding a rolled baby blanket or small pillow under your baby's head can be used if your arm is tired. Her head should be slightly higher than her tummy and rolled toward the breast.

Football Position

For nursing the right breast, stack pillows on your right side between you and the arm of your chair, or place a nursing pillow to your side. Slide your baby under your right arm and turn her on her side so her tummy is up against your ribs.

Be sure your baby is resting at nipple level. Hold the base of her head with your right hand and hold your right breast with your left hand in a "**U**" shape about **2 inches** behind the nipple.

Stroke your baby's lips up and down with your nipple and when she opens her mouth wide, bring her *quickly* to the breast using your hand behind her head. (See Tickle-Open-On pages 22–23)

To nurse the left breast, stack pillows on your left, hold baby's head with your left hand and support your left breast with your right hand.

Avoid placing your baby on his back and tilting his head forward as this can cause a shallow latch and make it hard for your baby to swallow.

A Good Latch

Your baby's mouth should be wide open with lips curled out. The nipple and about **1 inch** of tissue around the nipple should be in your baby's mouth.

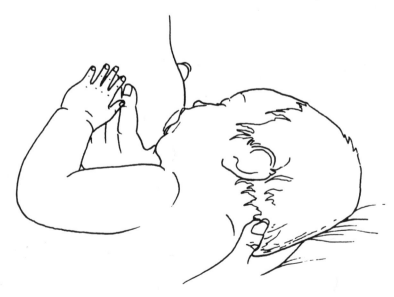

If your baby's lips are curled in, the baby is on just the nipple or if the nipple hurts, take your baby off the breast and try again.

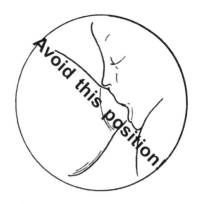

How To Take Baby off the Breast

Be sure your hands are clean and your fingernails are trimmed. Slide your index finger or pinkie into the corner of your baby's mouth to break suction. Feel for the lower gum and pull down on the gum to open his jaw while taking baby from the breast. Pulling your baby off your breast without opening his jaw first can cause nipple soreness and pain.

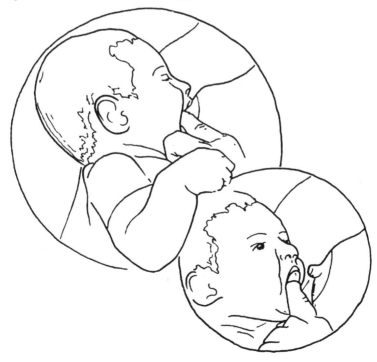

When baby comes off the breast after a *good* latch, the nipple should be slightly longer and round.

If you see creasing or wedging of the nipple or cracks, scabs, or blisters it may mean that your baby has a poor latch (not enough of the breast in the baby's mouth).

Common Pitfalls

1. Do *not* lean forward to place your breast in your baby's mouth. Always bring your baby to you.

2. Do *not* use your nipple to pry your baby's mouth open. Continue to tickle his lips and be patient for a wide-open response.

3. Do *not* try all positions at once. Use what works best in the first few days. Once you and your baby have learned to "latch-on," then try new positions.

3

How Often and How Long?

When do I start? How often do I nurse and for how long? And how will I know if my baby is getting enough?

Begin to nurse your baby as soon after delivery as possible. Your baby will likely be very alert for the first 2 hours after birth. This is a great time for you both to begin.

You may have noticed colostrum leaking from your nipple at the end of your pregnancy. Colostrum is thick, may look yellow or clear, and is full of antibodies and nutrients. It is good for your baby and helps start bowel movements sooner.

Newborns should be nursed on demand, that is, when they show signs of being hungry. On average they will nurse about **8 to 12 times** in 24 hours. Signs of hunger include smacking lips or sucking tongue, moving fist toward mouth or chewing on fingers, or body motions with vocal noises.

Crying is a late sign of hunger and usually means your baby's earlier signals have been missed. Your baby will be more upset and it will be harder to get her latched on once she is crying, so try to notice when your baby is just starting to get hungry. Your baby's schedule may be easy to predict but more likely it will vary, so watch for the early signs of hunger.

Rather than feeding at set times, breastfed babies often "cluster feed." This means they may want to feed **3 or 4 times** in a row at 1 to 1½ hours apart. These feedings may be short. This cluster of feedings is often followed by a 2- or 3-hour rest. *This is normal.* This cluster

> Feedings are timed from the start of one feed to the start of the next feed.

feeding pattern allows your baby to "tank up" his tummy. It usually occurs before or after your baby has been sleeping for a long time. Do not try to put your baby on a schedule by either the length of the feedings or the frequency of the feedings as this can cause problems with your milk supply and baby's weight gain. The time between each feeding will get longer as your baby gets older and his tummy grows. But for at least the first 2 to 3 months, plan to feed him often.

If your baby sleeps a lot during the day, he may want to eat more during the night to catch up. If you feed your baby often during the day and evening, he is more likely to sleep a little longer during the night. So during the first 4 to 6 weeks you may want to wake your baby during the day to offer a feeding if it has been three hours since the last one.

How long should a nursing session last?

Focus on finishing the first breast rather than the number of minutes it will take. The amount of milk in the breast and your baby's eagerness will change from feeding to feeding. Since the type of milk your baby gets changes from the beginning of the feeding to the end of the feeding, it is

> It is important to finish one breast before starting the other.

important to finish one breast before starting the other.

Allow your baby to nurse the first breast until swallow sounds (a swallow every **1 to 3 sucks**) are heard less often (a swallow every **7 to 8 sucks**). Swallows are soft, throaty noises although sometimes gulping can be heard. You will know your baby has finished the first side when these swallow changes occur and the whole breast softens to the touch.

Be sure to check the breast area near the armpit and underneath the breast for softening, as these are the areas of the breast that are harder to empty. Feedings can be as brief as **7 or 8 minutes** or as long as **25 minutes** or more. When finished, your baby will often let go of the nipple or fall asleep content. Your baby may

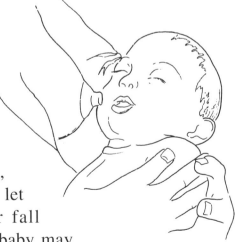

allow the last mouthful of milk to flow from the corner of his mouth.

The milk you make at the start of the feeding, **foremilk,** is higher in sugars and will look thinner. **Hindmilk** is made later in the feeding and is higher in fat and amino acids. It looks thicker and creamier.

Because the nutrients and calorie content of your breastmilk changes during the feeding, it is important to have your baby nurse one side fully rather than both sides partly. So, **finish the first breast first.** Give your baby a chance to burp and then offer the second breast. The second side is dessert and is optional. Many babies are one-sided nursers so your baby may be full after the first breast. At some feeds your baby may want some or all of the milk from the second breast as well.

Switch which breast you start with at each feeding. Don't worry about "keeping them even." It is common for one breast to make a little more milk than the other and for the breasts to be slightly uneven in shape or size.

Your baby will change between a stronger "tug" suck and a softer "flutter" suck, which feels more like she is flicking the nipple with her tongue. The tug suck pulls most of the milk from the breast. The flutter suck is used to start "let down" and to pacify or soothe your baby. Don't worry about your baby using the breast as a "pacifier." This is normal. (Artificial pacifiers became popular when babies were mainly bottle fed and could not get enough suck time in during bottle feeds.)

Is My Baby Getting Enough?

Although you cannot see how much milk your baby is taking in, there are ways to know that she is getting enough.

- Your baby should have *at least* **8 feedings** in a 24-hour period during the first several weeks.

- Your breasts should feel full before a feeding and soften to the touch after the feeding.

- You should hear frequent swallows during the first several minutes of nursing (a swallow with every **1 to 3 sucks**).

Common Myths

- Holding off feedings because frequent feedings are seen as "snacks" or a bad habit.

- Switching baby from one breast to the other after a given time so they are kept "even."

- Believing all time spent at breast is active feed time with lots of milk swallowed.

- Your baby should have **6 to 8 urine (wet or pee) diapers** in a 24-hour period by the time she is one week old. Urine should be clear to light yellow in color. Dark urine or "brick red" spots in the diaper could indicate your baby is not getting enough milk. Babies less than one week old may put out only about as many wet diapers as they are days old. *This is fine* as long as they are nursing well and the urine is not dark yellow in color. Watch that this number grows (use feeding and diaper log in section 11) each day as he approaches one week of age. It's hard to tell the urine content with disposable diapers. Lining the diaper with a tissue or gauze square will help you count baby's wet diapers.

- Your baby's stool (poop) should turn from black meconium to greenish-brown transitional and then to yellow "milk" stool by the time your baby is 5 days old. The stool will be thin and often look like watered-down yellow mustard. It may also look seedy or clumpy like cottage cheese. Your baby may have several small stools per day or 1 or 2 large ones. The total amount of stool in 24 hours should be at least enough to fill the cupped palm of your hand (a scoop of poop), about two tablespoons. Many babies have fewer stools per day as they get older, but the total amount of stool in 24 hours should be at least a "scoop of poop" per day. If the amount is less than this or the stool has not turned yellow by day 5 this may mean that your baby is not getting enough milk.

- Babies should lose no more than 7 percent to 8 percent of their birth weight. By nursing often from day 1, too much weight loss (10 percent or more) should not occur. Babies should regain their birth weight by 2 weeks of age and should continue to gain a minimum of ½ to 1 ounce per day for the first few months.

- Your baby's mouth should look moist and her tongue should be covered with clear saliva. Thick, pasty, white saliva or a dry tongue could mean your baby is not getting enough milk.

- Keep a log of your baby's feedings, and wet and dirty diapers for the first few weeks. This will give you a better idea of whether she is getting enough to eat. See the easy-to-use log sheets starting on page 77.

4

Engorgement

This section covers common problems some mothers experience and clearly explains the steps to take to help solve them.

Primary Engorgement

As your milk production changes from colostrum to "early" milk, then to mature milk, your breasts will also go through changes.

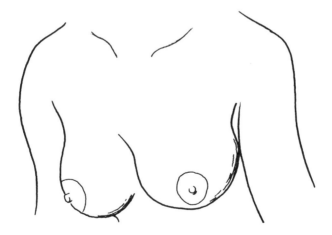

They will become larger, firmer and warmer to the touch. This is caused by some tissue swelling and a small amount of milk. This usually occurs 2

to 3 days after your baby is born and usually lasts 24 to 36 hours. This is called **primary engorgement.**

If you or your baby are not able to breastfeed within the first 24 hours, the milk production process may be delayed by a couple of days. If you have had a caesarean section, ask for help in finding a comfortable position so you may begin breastfeeding as soon as possible. If your baby is ill and unable to breastfeed, begin pumping your breasts within 24 hours of delivery.

Women who try pumping for long periods find that the firmness remains and very little milk comes out. Such long pumping sessions are *not* a good idea.

Resolving Primary Engorgement

For your comfort and to make a good milk supply; NURSE YOUR BABY OFTEN (at least **every 2 hours**). Before each feeding cover the breast with very warm wet towels for 3 to 5 minutes to increase milk flow. After each feeding place a cool compress to the breast (such as frozen peas in a plastic bag) for about 20 minutes. This is done for comfort and to reduce swelling.

This phase of engorgement can cause the breast to become tight and the nipple to flatten. This may cause your baby to have a hard time latching on even though he had been nursing well before engorgement

occurred. To help your baby latch on, use a warm wet towel as described above and then hand-express enough milk so that the nipple and areola are compressible or "squishy" between your thumb and index finger.

To hand-express, massage your breasts for a minute or two in small circles as in a self-breast exam. Then place your thumb on your breast above the nipple and your fingers below the nipple, about 1½ to 2 inches behind the nipple. Gently press your thumb and fingers toward each other, as you slide them toward the nipple. This should allow milk to flow from the nipple.

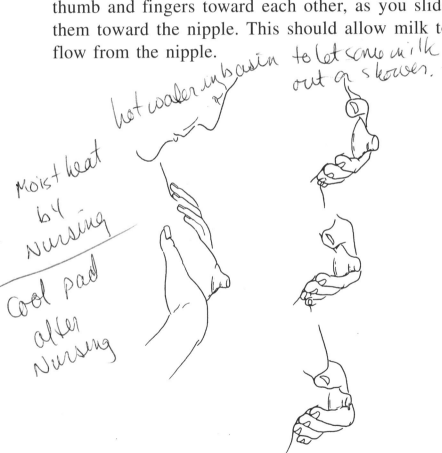

Hand-expression technique

The rest of the breast will remain full and firm. Frequent nursing sessions will soften the breasts. You will then notice that the breasts will soften a lot after a feeding and become full again as you approach the next feeding time. The longer the time between feedings the more full your breasts will get.

Secondary Engorgement

Secondary engorgement can occur at any time during lactation and is due to a large volume of milk in the breast. It is often caused by skipped or delayed feedings. Skipped or delayed feedings may come from changes in the baby's feeding pattern or by skipping a feeding when weaning. The point at which a woman feels engorged depends on her own milk production and the size of her breasts. Frequent or severe engorgement can lead to a decreased milk supply, plugged ducts, or mastitis (breast infection), so avoid this.

Resolving Secondary Engorgement

If you wish to continue to breastfeed, cover the breast with very warm wet towels for a few minutes and get baby to nurse out milk as soon as possible. If you are away from your baby you may need a double, electric, hospital-grade breast pump to do this.

If you are trying to wean your production or if your baby is dropping feedings, then use hand expression or an effective breast pump to remove enough milk to get comfortable. Do NOT empty your breast completely unless you have a plugged duct or mastitis (see section 6). Engorgement will stop when your milk production decreases to your baby's needs.

Leaking

Leaking can occur at any time during lactation. Some women leak colostrum during the end of pregnancy. Since the muscles in the nipple that surround the small openings function better in some women than others, some women have less leaking than others.

Frequent leaking should slow down or stop after the first 6 weeks of breastfeeding as your milk supply comes in line with your baby's demand and the small muscles at the openings in your nipple become more toned. Leaking occurs by triggering the "let-down response." This can happen when your breasts are full, hearing a baby cry, thinking of your baby or even just having pressure on your chest, such as with a front baby carrier or when carrying grocery bags.

Over-stimulation of the nipple can also cause leaking. The over-stimulation can come from short very frequent nursings, sexual activity, or prolonged use of breast shells that are used to pull out inverted nipples.

If leaking is a problem, try to avoid short, very frequent nursings. Also avoid using breast shells and limit nipple stimulation during sexual activity. In addition, try to avoid having your breasts get over-full from missing feeds. When missed or late feedings occur, nurse as soon as possible, hand-express or use an effective breast pump to fully empty your breasts.

A poorly fitting or tight bra can also place too much pressure on the breasts and cause leaking. Be sure to be properly fitted for a nursing bra during your early weeks of nursing.

Leaking during the night can come from pressure placed on the breasts with sleep positions. Try to nurse just before going to bed and either wear nursing pads or simply place a towel on the bed.

Nursing pads come in disposable or washable forms. If you choose disposable, be sure there is no plastic liner on the pad as the plastic can trap moisture and cause nipple breakdown. Some women prefer to use handkerchiefs or cut-up cloth diapers. Do not use cut up disposable diapers as these have a plastic backing and may contain a gel for absorbing urine. Some of that gel could remain on your breast when you remove the diaper to feed your baby.

Breast shells that are used to pull out inverted nipples should be used during the last trimester of pregnancy. Don't use them if you are at risk for preterm (early) labor because they can cause you to have contractions.

Medela Softshells®
Inverted Breast Shells

Once milk production begins these shells will cause leaking as the slight suction on the breast meant to draw out your nipple will also draw out your milk. To pull out inverted nipples after lactation has begun, roll the nipple with your fingers, or use a good breast pump.

A lot of leaking or leaking beyond the first six weeks can mean poor emptying of the breast by the baby or an overproduction of breastmilk. You should contact a lactation consultant, a La Leche League Leader or your health-care provider for more help.

To help limit leaking while your body is getting used to what your baby needs, nurse or use a good breast pump before you go out or exercise and before your breasts overfill. Wear layered, loose-fitting clothing, such as a T-shirt with a loose blouse over it. Wear patterned fabrics, rather than solids, to hide wet stains. And double up on your bra pads and change them often.

Firmly pressing the heel of your hand against your nipples for a minute or two can also help stop sudden leaking. However, because this is the body's way of releasing excess milk when overfilling occurs, if you do this often you can cause a plugged duct.

5

Sore Nipples

Sore nipples are often a sign of a poor latch-on. What to look for and what to avoid.

Nipple soreness, a common complaint in early breastfeeding, is only normal as you begin each feeding in the first few days. If your nipples continue to be sore during or between feedings, they are cracked, bleeding, scabbed, blistered, or have a creased shape to them after a nursing, there might be a latch-on problem that should be corrected. Nipple soreness can also be caused by thrush (see section 5) or tongue-tie (see your baby's doctor).

Long or frequent feeds don't cause nipple soreness. Shortening feeds will only delay soreness and will also interfere with making a good milk supply. Nipple tissue is *not* callus-forming and *will not* toughen up.

A poor latch-on may be due to not enough of the nipple and areola in the baby's mouth. Sometimes baby's tongue may be pulled back behind the lower gum or the latch is higher on one side of the nipple than on the other. Poor removal from the breast (see section 1) can also cause nipple damage.

gel pads –
can put in fridge

Lanolin creams or gel dressings are often used to soothe sore nipples. They help heal, but do not fix the latch-on problem. A poor latch can break down nipple tissue faster than any cream or gel dressing could heal it. Sore nipples are probably the most common cause for giving up on breastfeeding, yet are usually fixed with a little bit of help. Seek the help of a lactation consultant or a La Leche League Leader as soon as possible.

Breast shells that allow air to flow around and keep clothing off very sore nipples can be soothing as well, but also do not help the latch-on problem.

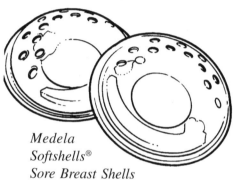

Medela Softshells®
Sore Breast Shells

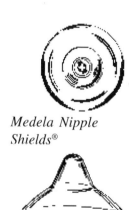

Medela Nipple Shields®

Nipple shields can be used as a last resort. Ask your lactation consultant or La Leche League Leader how to use them because they can decrease the amount of milk the baby gets. This lowers your milk supply and your baby may not gain as much weight. Nipple shields, like shells, lanolin, and gel dressings, only treat the symptoms and do not fix the latch-on problem.

⤷ *what I saw*
at LLL

6

Jaundice

Many newborns become jaundiced for one reason or another. This section describes the different types of jaundice, how to prevent it and how to continue to breastfeed if it does occur.

Jaundice or yellow coloring to your baby's skin and the whites of his eyes is caused by an excess amount of bilirubin in your baby's blood. During pregnancy your baby needs extra red blood cells in his body. After birth, these extra red blood cells break down and produce bilirubin. Bilirubin is filtered from your baby's body through his liver and by stooling. There are four types of jaundice.

Physiologic Jaundice
This is the most common cause for jaundice in a newborn. It begins to appear when your baby is 2 to 3 days old. It can last for about 10 days to 2 weeks. Because newborns have immature livers, the amount of bilirubin they can filter is limited. The excess in the blood causes the baby to look yellow (jaundiced).

Bilirubin will pass through the stool (poop) as well. If the stool remains in the intestines for any length of time, the bilirubin will reabsorb into the baby's bloodstream and increase the bilirubin level or delay the time it takes to resolve his jaundice.

Pathologic Jaundice

This type of jaundice is more rare. It appears in the first 24 hours after birth. It is due to a blood type or Rh incompatibility between mother and baby or liver disease. This type of jaundice can become severe and your baby will be treated more quickly than for other types of jaundice.

Breastmilk Jaundice

This type of jaundice occurs about 5 days to 2 weeks after birth and can last for up to 2 to 3 months. This type of jaundice occurs because a substance in breastmilk may interfere with the ability of your baby's liver to process bilirubin. It rarely elevates to a level needing treatment.

Breastfeeding Jaundice

This type of jaundice occurs because your baby is NOT breastfeeding enough. He may not be feeding often enough or his technique is poor. Occasionally mom's milk supply is low.

Because moms and babies are discharged 1 to 3 days after birth, jaundice may occur at home. If your baby appears jaundiced to you, be sure to contact your baby's doctor right away.

Preventing Jaundice

- Do not offer water or formula feeds as long as you have a good milk supply and if your baby is feeding at least 8 to 12 times a day and has a sufficient number of wet and dirty diapers.

- Finish the first breast first to be sure your baby is getting plenty of hindmilk.

- Breastfeed your baby as soon after birth as possible (preferably within the first 2 hours).

- Breastfeed your baby often, at least 8 to 12 times in 24 hours.

These techniques will allow your baby to stool early and often, which is an important part in getting rid of bilirubin from his body.

Jaundice Treatment

It is important to treat jaundice to prevent your baby's bilirubin level from getting too high. A very high bilirubin level can cause permanent damage to your baby's brain and nervous system.

- Your baby may need to have "light treatments" known as phototherapy to help filter the bilirubin from his body. Your baby will need to be fed often, every 2 to 3 hours while receiving phototherapy to avoid dehydration and to help flush out bilirubin from his body.

- Your baby may be sleepy and more difficult to wake to feed while he is jaundiced. It is important to wake your baby to feed at least every 2 to 3 hours to make sure he will get enough calories and fluids to help reduce jaundice.

To Wake a Sleepy Baby:

- Undress him down to his T-shirt and diaper unless your room is very cool.

- Lower the lights in the room.

- Talk to him.

- Gently rub his back or feet.

- Wash his face with a cool cloth.

If your baby remains too sleepy to get at least 8 to 10 good feeds in 24 hours, call your baby's doctor.

7

Thrush

Thrush is a yeast infection that can be treated with medication. This section teaches you the steps to follow in addition to the medication to reduce the chance of reinfection.

Sore nipples can also come from a yeast infection on the nipple known as thrush. This causes the nipple to look reddened and shiny. After a feeding the nipple may itch and burn. Sometimes the tissue around the nipple peels. Your baby may have white patches on the inside of his cheek, on his tongue or inside his lower lip. He may have a diaper rash that is red, shiny and peeling.

This condition needs medical treatment for mom and baby because the organism, candida, which causes thrush, is transferred back and forth during feeds.

Your doctor, midwife, lactation consultant, or La Leche League Leader can tell if you or your baby has thrush. But you will need to get the prescriptions needed for treatment from your doctor or midwife. Your lactation consultant or a La Leche League Leader can be very helpful to you with the daily care of thrush.

Missing

Daily Care of Thrush

Thrush infections can be difficult to get rid of since reinfection is common. In addition to prescription medication, stick to the following cleanliness procedures for two weeks. Following these steps will help reduce the chance for reinfection and prolonged treatment.

• The medicine given to your baby works only on contact with the patches in your baby's mouth. It will work better if you transfer the dose to a clean paper cup and use a cotton swab (Q-Tip) to coat the surfaces of your baby's mouth with the medicine. If you use a dropper in your baby's mouth, you may miss areas. And the rest of the medicine could become contaminated if you put the dropper back in the bottle. Be sure to continue to use the medication for **2 weeks** even if the white patches go away before then.

• Items that come in contact with the baby's mouth or your milk should be boiled for **20 minutes** once each day. This includes items such as pacifiers, bottle nipples, breast shells and breast pump parts.

• Milk pumped during a thrush infection can contain the candida organism, which can cause reinfection of your baby when the milk is thawed and fed to your baby later on. Freezing will not kill this organism. Do not store milk more than 24 hours while being treated for thrush.

• Wash your hands well with warm soapy water after handling your breasts, breastmilk, touching your baby's mouth or changing your baby's diaper. Use paper towels for drying since damp cloth towels can grow yeast.

- Change your bra pads after each feeding and use a clean bath towel and bra each day.

- Wash towels and clothing that come in contact with breastmilk in very hot water (greater than 122° F, 50° C) to kill the yeast.

- Rinse your nipples after feeds with a vinegar and water solution (1 tablespoon of white vinegar to 2 cups of water) to help soothe the nipples. Pat dry with a paper towel then apply prescription cream.

- You can have your doctor prescribe the cream version of the baby's medication that will coat your nipples better than putting the baby's medication on your nipples. The liquid medication can be messy and sticky as it contains sugar. Be sure to continue the medication to your nipples for 2 weeks even if your nipples feel better before then. Stopping the medication for your nipples or your baby's mouth too soon can allow the thrush to regrow.

8

Plugged Ducts and Mastitis

Retained milk in the breast can lead to a plug forming in the duct. Unresolved plugged ducts can lead to mastitis, a breast infection. This section covers the steps to help unblock plugged ducts and identifies the symptoms and treatment of mastitis.

A plugged duct refers to an area in the breast that has become blocked by the solid parts of the milk. Further milk production is unable to flow forward and creates a "pool" of milk behind the "plug." This can occur from delayed or poor emptying of the breast or by pressures from a front baby carrier, a poorly fitting bra, or a sleep position. Sometimes, scarring from previous breast surgery prevents the breast from emptying fully. Excessive stress or fatigue are the most common reasons for plugged ducts as they can hinder letdown and therefore prevent adequate emptying of the breast.

A plugged duct causes the breast to feel full and firm in an area that is also tender to the touch. You may be able to feel a lump in the breast the size of a small pea or grape or even larger. Sometimes the plug is much deeper in the breast and harder to locate.

To help resolve a plugged duct, apply very warm wet towels to the breast for **3 to 5 minutes** before each feeding and massage this area, from the plug toward the nipple, during the feeding. Nurse your baby more often and start with this breast at each feeding. You may need to repeat this process a few times to unplug the duct.

During a feeding, position your baby so that her chin is facing in the direction of the plug. This may help to more completely empty that area of the breast. Sometimes a persistent plug can be dislodged by following a good feeding session with another warm water soak and pumping with a double electric hospital grade breast pump for about **10** minutes while massaging the areas around the plug.

Unresolved plugged ducts can lead to a breast infection called mastitis. Be persistent with attempts to resolve the plugging. Call a lactation consultant, a La Leche League Leader or your doctor for help if you have questions or need help.

Mastitis

Mastitis, also know as a breast inflammation or infection, can be caused by plugged ducts but are often caused by being very tired. Mastitis can occur throughout lactation. The symptoms include headache, chills, fever, general achiness, and a tender breast with a warm pink to reddened area. It is important to have this treated quickly. It is *perfectly fine* to breastfeed during mastitis. The milk is *not* affected and if antibiotics are needed, ask your doctor for one that is safe for use while breastfeeding. It is important to have the breast emptied on a regular basis, preferably by your baby but a good quality, double, electric hospital-grade breast pump can be used as a back up. Very warm wet towels should be applied before feeding or pumping and massage the affected area during the feeding. Drink plenty of fluids and get plenty of rest to get rid of the mastitis.

If you are started on antibiotics, it is important to finish them even if you are feeling better as antibiotics taken for fewer than 10 to 14 days are linked with the infection coming back.

9

Do I Need to Use a Breast Pump?

Women who choose to pump do so for a number of reasons. How to prepare and what pump is best for your needs are covered in this section.

If your baby is having trouble nursing, you may need to use a breast pump right away. You may also want to use one later on, even if breastfeeding is going well but you would like or need your baby to take a bottle. Many moms choose not to pump at all. They do not need or wish to have their baby take a bottle and continue to breastfeed until their babies are weaned. Some moms hand-express for adding breastmilk to their baby's cereal.

If you feel you will need to offer a bottle at any point in the future, 4 to 6 weeks of age is the best time to introduce one. If you offer a bottle nipple sooner, it may interfere with your baby's ability to latch-on correctly (known as "nipple confusion") or your baby may develop a preference for the faster flow of the bottle nipple. If you wait until your baby is 3 or 4 months old, he may not want to take anything but the breast.

Sometimes it is necessary to offer your baby supplemental feeds of pumped breastmilk or even formula while breastfeeding problems are being solved. These feeds can be offered using feeding devices other than baby bottles to keep your baby nourished because bottle feeding can sometimes interfere with latching on. Your lactation consultant or La Leche League Leader will help you in choosing the methods best for you and your baby.

Women pump for many reasons: to offer breastmilk to their baby if they are out and are shy about nursing in public (although I encourage women to nurse in public as breastfeeding is a normal and natural event), returning to work, or to help build or maintain a milk supply while a breastfeeding problem is being solved.

The type of pump you choose will depend on your reason for pumping. For this reason it is not a good idea to purchase pumps before the baby is born. Double, electric hospital-grade pumps allow you to pump both breasts at the same time. They help build or maintain milk supply over a short time and for regular pumping mixed with breastfeeding for a long time.

> Pumping both breasts at the same time not only saves you time, but it increases your milk production by raising your prolactin level. Prolactin is the hormone that is responsible for milk production.

Breast pumps are classified by how fast they pump (cycling) and how strong they pump (suctioning). A double electric hospital-grade pump will cycle about 48 times per minute and suction up to 240 to 250mm of pressure. This level is similar to a baby nursing.

Battery-grade pumps suction fewer times per minute and reach lower maximum levels of suction than double, electric hospital-grade pumps. Pumps in the battery-grade category can vary greatly in ability and performance. This slower pumping speed and suction level is less efficient at removing milk than the double electric pump. Therefore they are useful

Medela Mini-Electric®

only for a mom with an already established milk supply and then, only for occasional pumping (2 to 3 times per week). Since the motor is relatively small, heavy use will burn it out quickly. Some battery-grade pumps can be plugged into an electric outlet, and may be labeled an "electric pump," but that will not change their effectiveness.

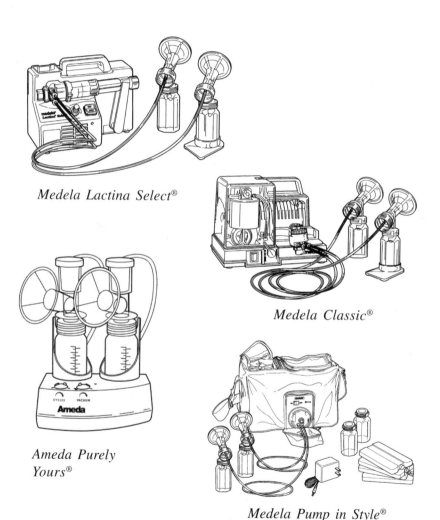

Medela Lactina Select®

Medela Classic®

Ameda Purely Yours®

Medela Pump in Style®

Manual pumps can be useful sometimes. Proper instruction on how to use a manual pump (or any pump for that matter), makes a big difference in how well it works. Some pumps let you change the flange or breast funnel to a larger size. Since breasts come in all shapes, sizes, and textures this is an important feature that makes a big difference in how well the pump works for you and how comfortable it feels.

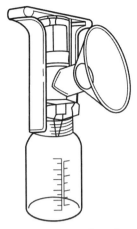

Ameda One-hand Breast Pump®

Many moms find that lower-end pumps, available in many baby stores and drugstores, are ineffective at milk removal and can cause nipple soreness. Contact a lactation consultant, a La Leche League Leader or a pump rental station to help you choose which kind of pump will work best for your needs.

More and more women are choosing to pump and feed breastmilk in a bottle and not breastfeed their babies. Although this time-consuming option provides your baby with the benefits of breastmilk, some of the benefits of breastfeeding are lost or decreased. The body seems to know the difference between a baby nursing and a pump. After a certain length of time (3 to 6 months) the body will begin to decrease production no matter how good the quality of your pump.

Exclusively pumping is often the result of frustration over unresolved nursing problems. Seek the help of a lactation consultant or La Leche League Leader at the first sign of breastfeeding problems. Don't wait until you and your family are stressed out by breastfeeding problems. Call the experts right away. You will be more successful and more relaxed if you get help early.

Not all problems are fixed in a short period of time. Some may take several weeks. Some parents may decide to pump and feed breastmilk in a bottle if they haven't been able to solve their breastfeeding problem. Remember, breastmilk in any container is still the best food for your baby.

10

Pumping and Storage of Milk

How to build a milk bank, manage replacement feedings, properly store and reheat pumped milk are addressed in this section.

Pumping To Build a Milk Bank

If you are trying to build a milk bank for spare bottles while your baby is nursing for all feedings:

If your baby nurses both breasts per feeding you can double-pump your breasts for about **10 minutes** after you have nursed the baby to collect any remaining milk. You may get only small amounts, about 1 ounce or so. You can do this a couple of times per day and add the pumpings together to get a full feeding. If it takes longer than 24 hours to collect an amount for a full feeding you can freeze the first day's milk, then chill the milk collected on subsequent days in the refrigerator before adding it to the frozen milk. When the amount of milk collected in the frozen bottle is enough for a full feeding, start a new collection bottle.

If your baby nurses one breast per feeding you can pump out the other breast for about **15 minutes** and store the milk for later use. To save time, some women pump one breast while their babies feed on the other.

As your baby gets older there will be a gap in nighttime feedings long enough for you to add one extra pumping at the end of the day. For example, your baby nurses last at 8:00 P.M. You pump about 10:00 P.M. or 11:00 P.M. and your baby doesn't wake for next feed until about 6:00 A.M.

Pumping for Replacement Feedings

If you are pumping for a replacement feeding (you are pumping instead of nursing your baby), such as when you go back to work or school, you will want to double pump for 15 to 20 minutes at about the same time you would have nursed your baby. If your baby is older and doesn't need to feed as often, or if your workday is shorter than average, you may need to pump only once. If your baby is younger, feeding often, or your workday is longer than average, you will need to pump more often. Nursing your baby just before you leave in the morning and when you get home will limit the number of pumpings needed. As your baby gets older and doesn't need to feed as often or when solid foods have been added at about 6 months of age, you will be able to decrease the number of times you pump.

Storage and Reheating of Milk

Your milk can be stored either in plastic or glass baby bottles or in milk storage bags. It is best to pump, store and feed breastmilk from the same container as this avoids pouring milk from one container to another, which can cause spillage, contamination or loss of some beneficial nutrients that can cling to the sides of the container.

Baby bottles come in two different kinds of plastic: a cloudy, softer plastic and a clear hard plastic. The clear hard plastic scratches more easily and leaves ridges that can increase bacterial growth and allow more of the nutrients in breastmilk to cling to the sides of the bottle. The cloudy, softer plastic is better for storing breastmilk.

Breastmilk can also be stored in disposable bottle liners also known as milk storage bags. The bags designed for breastmilk are made of a thicker plastic that limit the chance of odors and bacteria getting into to the milk. They can usually be attached to a breast pump in place of a bottle, eliminating the need to

Medela CSF Bags®

pour your milk. Bottle liners made for formula can be used, but need to be doubled (place one bag inside another) to increase their strength and to keep odors and bacteria from getting into the breastmilk. These cannot be hooked onto your breast pump. You will need to pump into a bottle and pour into these liners for storing. These are less expensive but harder to use.

Bottles should be stored with either a one-piece cap or two-piece systems called collars and discs. These form a better seal than using the bottle nipple and dome lid as a cap. The better seal helps keep odors and  bacteria from getting into the milk and prevents leakage if the bottle tips over. The rubber nipple may wear out more quickly when it is cleaned and stored in very hot or cold temperatures.

Breastmilk is storable in the refrigerator for 8 days at 32° to 39° Fahrenheit, or in the freezer for 3 to 4 months at 0° Fahrenheit. Milk in the freezer should be stored in the middle of the freezer and on a rack. Milk placed in contact with the floor or sides of the freezer can spoil more quickly because contact with automatic defrost cycles can cause partial defrosting and refreezing. Milk stored in the door of the freezer or toward the front is subject to large temperature changes each time the freezer is opened and closed.

Expressed breastmilk is stable at room temperature (66° to 72°) for up to 10 hours. If you are not going to use the milk right away, refrigerate it or surround it with cold packs if you are going to take it with you. If the milk is stored at a temperature above 72°, the milk will spoil in less than 10 hours.

Bottle rack systems that allow for older milk to be used first are handy. Always date your stored milk (refrigerated or frozen) so you can easily rotate your supply.

Breastmilk storage guidelines

Type	Room temperature 66°–72° F	Refrigerator 32°–39°F	Home freezer Appx. 0°	Deep freezer 0° or less
Expressed breast milk	10 hours	8 days	3–4 months if frozen within 24 hours.	6+ months
Previously frozen and thawed	1 hour	24 hours	Do not refreeze thawed milk	Do not refreeze thawed milk

Source: La Leche League International

Reheating Breastmilk

You can reheat refrigerated breastmilk by placing the bottle or bottle liner into warm tap water for a few minutes. The milk does not need to be "warm to the touch." Taking the chill off and bringing the milk to "room temperature" are fine. If the breastmilk is frozen, you can either place it in the refrigerator overnight for use the next day or place it in warm tap water for several minutes for more immediate use. DO NOT allow milk to defrost slowly on the counter as this can allow bacteria to grow.

NEVER microwave breastmilk or place milk in boiling water as this can easily overheat the milk, burn your baby's mouth and destroy some of the nutrients present in the milk.

Bottle warmers may be sufficient for reheating, *but* read the instructions *first* because some require at least 4 ounces of milk in the bottle to avoid overheating.

11

Mom's Diet

What to eat, what to limit. A well-balanced diet is the key.

While you nurse your baby, you should eat a well-balanced diet with between 500 to 1,000 calories over your pre-pregnancy diet, if you began your pregnancy within your normal weight range. You may need less if you were overweight, and more if you were underweight. You may need to eat more if you are making a large volume of milk (more than 1 liter—33 ounces—a day). Eating when you are hungry is a good guide.

Because making milk uses about 940 calories per liter, weight loss during lactation is fairly easy. You should not lose more than a pound per week, however. Excessive weight loss may hurt your ability to maintain a good supply.

You should drink a variety of fluids including lots of water. A good guideline is to drink during each nursing session and whenever you are thirsty. A good indicator you are getting enough fluids is that your urine is clear to light yellow in color.

Limit the amount of high-calorie or sugar items that are of low nutrient value. These may make you feel full but will not contribute to an overall well-balanced diet.

The foods and liquids you consume while breastfeeding can affect the flavor of your milk. But this is a benefit to your baby. He will be more likely to accept a wide variety of table foods when he is ready for them since he has already been exposed to the many flavors in your family's diet. Unless you are malnourished, the amount you eat does not significantly affect the overall quality of your milk as your body pulls from stores of nutrients built over time to make your breastmilk. Having a poor diet, however, can make you more likely to get sick.

Cultural beliefs may suggest certain foods to eat or avoid while you are pregnant or lactating, but it is an old wives' tale that you need to drink milk to make milk.

Routine vitamin supplements are not necessary while breastfeeding, if you have a nutritious, well-balanced diet. If your diet is poor (mostly junk food), it is a good idea to continue to take prenatal vitamins or a multivitamin.

If you can't tolerate dairy products or don't eat them, then you might need a calcium supplement. If you are a vegan, you may need a vitamin B12 supplement.

Although it is not common, some foods and beverages you eat can cause your baby to have gas as they pass through your milk. You can tell if your baby is gassy if he is crying, has drawn-up legs and a desire to nurse often. Your baby may wish to suck often to help relieve his discomfort.

Your best method for identifying these foods is trial and error.

Medications such as stool softeners and antibiotics may also cause your baby to have gas or diarrhea. Caffeine, found in coffee, tea, colas and some medications, and a similar substance found in chocolate can cause your baby to be fussy. Newborns do not filter caffeine as quickly as adults so it can build up over time. It's a good idea to limit caffeine to 1 to 2 cups a day or use decaffeinated products. If you have questions about your diet, or have special needs, ask your doctor, La Leche League Leader, lactation consultant or a registered dietitian for help.

12

Medications

When taking medications, ask your doctor if they are compatible with breastfeeding.

Medications generally transfer into breastmilk more quickly than food and are usually filtered out faster as well. Always consult your doctor, pharmacist or lactation consultant before taking any medication while breastfeeding. This includes prescription and over-the-counter medications.

Because a medication passes into your milk does not necessarily make it incompatible with breastfeeding. The amount and frequency taken and the manner in which that particular medication is filtered from your body will help determine how much medication is in your milk and whether that amount of that medication is potentially harmful to your baby. Please remind your doctor that you are breastfeeding whenever medications are being prescribed for you. Sometimes a different medication can still be effective without having to interrupt breastfeeding. Remember that over-the-counter medications should be checked for safety. Ask your doctor, pharmacist or lactation consultant for advice.

13

Baby's Feeding and Diaper Log

It is important to track the quantity of your baby's feedings, wet and dirty diapers, to know if your baby is getting enough milk. These log sheets will help you do that easily.

Days and nights run together when you are awake with your baby during the night. Without a good log sheet it is almost impossible to remember all this data, especially if you are not the only person changing diapers. Instruct everyone who may change the baby's diaper to mark the log sheet. Be sure to read the section titled "Is My Baby Getting Enough" starting on page 33.

The "feedings" and "wet diaper" counts are tracked with check marks. In the "dirty diapers" sections, shade in approximately how much stool (poop) your baby put out, with the desired range being an amount equal to what would fill the cupped palm of your hand (about 2 tablespoons) every 24 hours.

Check to verify that your results are in the shaded "desired" range. If you have any doubts, contact your pediatrician or a lactation consultant as soon as possible.

Baby's Feeding and Diaper Log: Week One

Day 1

			Desired
Feedings	☐1 ☐2 ☐3 ☐4 ☐5		☐6 ☐7 ☐8 ☐9 ☐10
Wet Diapers	☐1 ☐2		☐3 ☐4 ☐5
Dirty Diapers (tarry black)	None 1/2		1 — Cupped palm

Day 2

			Desired
Feedings	☐1 ☐2 ☐3 ☐4 ☐5 ☐6 ☐7		☐8 ☐9 ☐10 ☐11 ☐12
Wet Diapers	☐1 ☐2		☐3 ☐4 ☐5
Dirty Diapers (tarry black)	None 1/2		1 — Cupped palm

Day 3

			Desired
Feedings	☐1 ☐2 ☐3 ☐4 ☐5 ☐6 ☐7		☐8 ☐9 ☐10 ☐11 ☐12
Wet Diapers	☐1 ☐2		☐3 ☐4 ☐5 ☐6 ☐7 ☐8
Dirty Diapers (greenish-brown)	None 1/2		1 — Cupped palm

Day 4

			Desired
Feedings	☐1 ☐2 ☐3 ☐4 ☐5 ☐6 ☐7		☐8 ☐9 ☐10 ☐11 ☐12
Wet Diapers	☐1 ☐2 ☐3		☐4 ☐5 ☐6 ☐7 ☐8
Dirty Diapers (greenish-brown)	None 1/2		1 — Cupped palm

Day 5

			Desired
Feedings	☐1 ☐2 ☐3 ☐4 ☐5 ☐6 ☐7		☐8 ☐9 ☐10 ☐11 ☐12
Wet Diapers	☐1 ☐2 ☐3 ☐4		☐5 ☐6 ☐7 ☐8
Dirty Diapers (yellow seedy)	None 1/2		1 — Cupped palm

Day 6

			Desired
Feedings	☐1 ☐2 ☐3 ☐4 ☐5 ☐6 ☐7		☐8 ☐9 ☐10 ☐11 ☐12
Wet Diapers	☐1 ☐2 ☐3 ☐4 ☐5		☐6 ☐7 ☐8
Dirty Diapers (yellow seedy)	None 1/2		1 — Cupped palm

Day 7

			Desired
Feedings	☐1 ☐2 ☐3 ☐4 ☐5 ☐6 ☐7		☐8 ☐9 ☐10 ☐11 ☐12
Wet Diapers	☐1 ☐2 ☐3 ☐4 ☐5		☐6 ☐7 ☐8
Dirty Diapers (yellow seedy)	None 1/2		1 — Cupped palm

Baby's Feeding and Diaper Log: Week Two

Day 8													Desired				
	Feedings	☐ 1	☐ 2	☐ 3	☐ 4	☐ 5	☐ 6	☐ 7		☐ 8	☐ 9	☐ 10	☐ 11	☐ 12			
	Wet Diapers			☐ 1	☐ 2	☐ 3	☐ 4	☐ 5		☐ 6	☐ 7	☐ 8					
	Dirty Diapers (yellow seedy)		None		1/2					1		Cupped palm					

Day 9													Desired				
	Feedings	☐ 1	☐ 2	☐ 3	☐ 4	☐ 5	☐ 6	☐ 7		☐ 8	☐ 9	☐ 10	☐ 11	☐ 12			
	Wet Diapers			☐ 1	☐ 2	☐ 3	☐ 4	☐ 5		☐ 6	☐ 7	☐ 8					
	Dirty Diapers (yellow seedy)		None		1/2					1		Cupped palm					

Day 10													Desired				
	Feedings	☐ 1	☐ 2	☐ 3	☐ 4	☐ 5	☐ 6	☐ 7		☐ 8	☐ 9	☐ 10	☐ 11	☐ 12			
	Wet Diapers			☐ 1	☐ 2	☐ 3	☐ 4	☐ 5		☐ 6	☐ 7	☐ 8					
	Dirty Diapers (yellow seedy)		None		1/2					1		Cupped palm					

Day 11													Desired				
	Feedings	☐ 1	☐ 2	☐ 3	☐ 4	☐ 5	☐ 6	☐ 7		☐ 8	☐ 9	☐ 10	☐ 11	☐ 12			
	Wet Diapers			☐ 1	☐ 2	☐ 3	☐ 4	☐ 5		☐ 6	☐ 7	☐ 8					
	Dirty Diapers (yellow seedy)		None		1/2					1		Cupped palm					

Day 12													Desired				
	Feedings	☐ 1	☐ 2	☐ 3	☐ 4	☐ 5	☐ 6	☐ 7		☐ 8	☐ 9	☐ 10	☐ 11	☐ 12			
	Wet Diapers			☐ 1	☐ 2	☐ 3	☐ 4	☐ 5		☐ 6	☐ 7	☐ 8					
	Dirty Diapers (yellow seedy)		None		1/2					1		Cupped palm					

Day 13													Desired				
	Feedings	☐ 1	☐ 2	☐ 3	☐ 4	☐ 5	☐ 6	☐ 7		☐ 8	☐ 9	☐ 10	☐ 11	☐ 12			
	Wet Diapers			☐ 1	☐ 2	☐ 3	☐ 4	☐ 5		☐ 6	☐ 7	☐ 8					
	Dirty Diapers (yellow seedy)		None		1/2					1		Cupped palm					

Day 14													Desired				
	Feedings	☐ 1	☐ 2	☐ 3	☐ 4	☐ 5	☐ 6	☐ 7		☐ 8	☐ 9	☐ 10	☐ 11	☐ 12			
	Wet Diapers			☐ 1	☐ 2	☐ 3	☐ 4	☐ 5		☐ 6	☐ 7	☐ 8					
	Dirty Diapers (yellow seedy)		None		1/2					1		Cupped palm					

Sue Tiller

Baby's Feeding and Diaper Log: Week Three

Day 15

										Desired				
Feedings	1	2	3	4	5	6	7		8	9	10	11	12
Wet Diapers	1	2	3	4	5				6	7	8		
Dirty Diapers (yellow seedy)	None		1/2			1	Cupped palm						

Day 16

										Desired				
Feedings	1	2	3	4	5	6	7		8	9	10	11	12
Wet Diapers	1	2	3	4	5				6	7	8		
Dirty Diapers (yellow seedy)	None		1/2			1	Cupped palm						

Day 17

										Desired				
Feedings	1	2	3	4	5	6	7		8	9	10	11	12
Wet Diapers	1	2	3	4	5				6	7	8		
Dirty Diapers (yellow seedy)	None		1/2			1	Cupped palm						

Day 18

										Desired				
Feedings	1	2	3	4	5	6	7		8	9	10	11	12
Wet Diapers	1	2	3	4	5				6	7	8		
Dirty Diapers (yellow seedy)	None		1/2			1	Cupped palm						

Day 19

										Desired				
Feedings	1	2	3	4	5	6	7		8	9	10	11	12
Wet Diapers	1	2	3	4	5				6	7	8		
Dirty Diapers (yellow seedy)	None		1/2			1	Cupped palm						

Day 20

										Desired				
Feedings	1	2	3	4	5	6	7		8	9	10	11	12
Wet Diapers	1	2	3	4	5				6	7	8		
Dirty Diapers (yellow seedy)	None		1/2			1	Cupped palm						

Day 21

										Desired				
Feedings	1	2	3	4	5	6	7		8	9	10	11	12
Wet Diapers	1	2	3	4	5				6	7	8		
Dirty Diapers (yellow seedy)	None		1/2			1	Cupped palm						

Endnotes

[1] *Pediatrics*, Vol. 100, No. 6, December 1995, pp. 1035–1039, American Academy of Pediatrics: "Breastfeeding and the Use of Human Milk."

[2] Koutras, A. K., "Fecal Secretory Immunoglobulin A in Breast Milk vs. Formula Feeding in Early Infancy." *Journal of Pediatric Gastroenterology and Nutrition,* 1989.

[3] Duncan, B.; Ey, J.; Holberg, C. J.; Wright, A. L.; Martinez, F. D., Taussig, L. M. "Exclusive breast-feeding for at least 4 months protects against otitis media." *Pediatrics.* 1993; 91:86-872.

Saarinen, U. M. "Recurrent otitis media in breastfed infants." *ACTA Paediatrica Scandinavica,* 1982; 71:567

[4] Mitchell, E. A; Taylor, B. J.: Ford, R. P. K., et al. "Four modifiable and other major risk factors for cot death: the New Zealand study." *Journal of Paediatrics and Child Health,* 1992; 28 (supplement 1):S3–8.

Ford, R. P.; Taylor, B. J.; Mitchell, E. A.; Enright, S. A.; Stewart, A. W.; Becroft, D. M. Scragg, R.; Hassall, I. B.; Barry D. M.; and Allen, E. M., Community Paediatric Unit, Christchurch, New Zealand. "Breastfeeding and the risk of sudden infant death syndrome." *International Journal of Epidemiology*, Vol. 22, 885–890, 1993. International Epidemiological Association.

[5] Heacock, H. J.; Jeffrey, H. E.; Baker, J.; Page, M. "The influences of breast versus formula feeding on gastro-oesophageal reflux in healthy newborn infants. *Journal of Pediatric Gastroenterology and Nutrition*. 14; 41–46.

[6] Wright; A. L.; Holberg, C. J.; Taussig, L. M.; Martinez, F. D. "Relationship of infant feeding to recurrent wheezing at age 6 years." *Archives of Pediatrics and Adolescent Medicine*, July 1995; 149: 758–763

[7] Kramer, F. et al. "Breastfeeding reduces material lower-body fat." *Journal of American Dietetic Association*, 93: 429–33, 1993.

[8] Chua, S.; Arulkumaran, S.; Lim, I., et al. "Influence of breastfeeding and nipple stimulation on postpartum uterine activity. *British Journal of Obstetrics and Gynaecology*. 1994; 101: 804–805

[9] Zheng, T.; Duan, L.; Liu, Y.; et al. "Lactation reduces breast cancer risk in Shandong Province, China." *American Journal of Epidemiology*. 2000; 152: 1129–1135

Rosenblatt, K. A. and Thomas, D. B. "Lactation and the risk of epithelial ovarian cancer." The WHO Collaborative Study of Neoplasia and Steroid Contraceptives, *International Journal of Epidemiology*, Vol. 22, 192–197

[10] Kalwart, H. J., and Specker, B. L. "Bone mineral loss during lactation and recovery after weaning." *Obstetrics and Gynecology*, 1995; 86:26–32

Melton, L. J. III; Bryant, S. C.; Wahner, H. W.; O'Fallon, W. M.; Malkasian, G. D.; Judd, H. L.; Riggs, B. L. "Influence of breastfeeding and other reproductive factors on bone mass later in life." *Osteoporosis International*, 1993, March; 3 (2): 76–32

Resources for Breastfeeding Mothers

ILCA
International Lactation Consultant Association
A professional organization for International Board Certified Lactation Consultants (IBCLC). Professionally trained, credentialed and experienced consultants who provide breastfeeding assistance in a variety of settings: hospitals, doctor's offices, public health, and private practice. To find a board certified lactation consultant in your area, call (919) 782-5181 during business hours. Visit their Web site: www.ilca.org/

La Leche League
Largest breastfeeding support group in the United States. Provides breastfeeding information and support through monthly meetings and telephone counseling. La Leche League Leaders are experienced and accredited. To find a LLL Leader or support group in your area call: (847) 519-7730 or (800) LaLeche or visit their Web site: www.lalecheleague.org/

WIC
Women, Infants, and Children
Supplemental nutrition program funded by U.S. federal government for pregnant and breastfeeding women, their infants and children up to age five who qualify for assistance.

To find breastfeeding peer counselors in your area visit this Web site: www.fns.usda.gov/wic/ and click on "Contacts."

Medela
Medela provides breast pumps and breastfeeding supplies. To find a rental station or lactation consultant in your area call the Breastfeeding National Network (BNN) at (800) TELL-YOU (835-5968) or visit their Web site: www.medela.com/

Ameda
Ameda provides breast pumps and breastfeeding supplies. To find a rental station in your area visit their Web site: www.ameda.com/

Breastfeeding101.com
For additional copies of *Breastfeeding 101, visit:* www.Breastfeeding101.com/

Index

Note: Page numbers in italics refer to illustrations.

for plugged duct assistance, 56
for sleepy baby concerns, 50
for thrush assistance, 51, 53
for tongue-tie concerns, 45

E

Ear infections, 15
Emptying breast, 31–32, 43
Engorgement
    primary engorgement, 37–40
    resolving, 38–41
    secondary engorgement, 40–41

F

Feeding instincts, 19, 29
Feedings
    alternating breasts, 32
    cluster feedings, 30
    delaying, 38, 40, 41
    frequency of, 29–30, 33, 38, 40–41
    length of, 30–32
    log sheets for, 33, 35, 77–81
    missed feedings, 41
    myths about, 33
    number of, 33
    replacement feedings, 66–67
    satisfying baby, 31–33
    skipped feedings, 40
    and swallows, 31, 33
    waking baby for, 49–50
    and working, 66
    see also Breastmilk; Nursing sessions
Fluid intake, 71–72
"Flutter" suck, 32
Football position
    illustration of, *25*
    learning, 17
    left breast, 26
    right breast, 25–26
    techniques for, 25–26
Foremilk, 32

H

Hand expression, *39*, 39–41, 59
Hindmilk, 32
Hunger signs, 29–30

I

International Lactation Consultant Association (ILCA), 85
Inverted nipples, 41, 42

About the Author

Sue Tiller is a registered nurse and an International Board Certified Lactation Consultant. She has been assisting breastfeeding moms for twenty-five years. Tiller has been a speaker at several breastfeeding conferences, has been regional representative to the board of directors of the Internal Lactation Consultant Association (ILCA) and the co-vice president of the Lactation Consultant Association of Greater Washington. Tiller has a successful private practice in Northern Virginia, where she lives with her husband and three daughters.